Songs From The Universe

An Exploration of Expression

KATHERINE VILNROTTER

ISBN: 978-1-7357121-1-6

DEDICATION

This is dedicated to anyone who has ever felt the spark of creative energy flow through them… anyone who has felt connected to something bigger than themselves, to anyone who has allowed their heart to open just enough to let that beautiful heart energy shine out into the world, to anyone and everyone who has allowed themselves to be truly vulnerable in the only way that matters…to connect your heart with the heart of another, amplifying the energy and power of love. Not romantic love, universal love. The love that connects us all, whether we know it or not. The love that heals everything that needs healing.

This is equally dedicated to anyone who has not felt that connection yet, and to those who feel they may have lost it forever or think they are incapable of such a connection. Fear not! This connection is for everyone and IS everyone. No one can take that away from you. No hurt or pain can remove your ability to connect with that that is YOU! Keep going… keep looking for you… never give up on yourself and you too will experience the love and connection that is your birthright. Never lose hope.

You are your own Love Cure.

CONTENTS

FORWARD
(WRITTEN IN 2021)

Time is a tricky and infinitely fascinating thing. The 33 entries included in this book were completed and copyrighted in 2018. I experienced a hugely powerful internal push to get it all out, go through it, copyright it, and then as soon as I did that, the push was gone. It felt 'shelved' internally, and for a long time I wondered if perhaps it was not meant to be published.

Perhaps it was all so that I could go through the process and learn and grow from that alone. Then the following year I started on my next book, The Love Cure: Connecting Back to You, which was published in 2020. It was not until I received Thoth's final transmission for me in The Love Cure text that I truly understood what Songs From The Universe really was. As soon as I channeled that message (which I included here for your reference), I knew that Songs From The Universe was to come next! It finally made sense! The very expressions described in this excerpt were already documented and ready to be expressed! These expressions hold the imprint of a very intense time of my healing process, my inner growth, my self-discovery, and my learnings.

Looking back, I could not have expressed or even accessed these energies AFTER going through the process of channeling The Love Cure. Yet, they truly didn't have any context until The Love Cure was written. These songs of my soul would have been lost to time, mere whispers in the wind of the Universe. Yet, I was guided to capture them before I moved on, preserving them in these words, for you, for me.

Time. Ever mysterious. Always divine.

I hope you enjoy the following excerpt from The Love Cure: Connecting Back to You (2020)…

…as well as the following 33 Songs From The Universe.

Remember, you are and always will be The Love Cure.

EXCERPT FROM THE LOVE CURE (2020)

THOTH

THE EXPRESSION

Some Context:

Whenever I am fearful about sharing something inside of me with the world, or even just with someone I love, whenever I start to judge myself, or my thoughts, or my feelings, or my creations, I read this again. There is no wrong way to express your deepest essence, which is pure Love. When Love emerges, in all of its glorious and beautiful ways, it is perfect. Even if it is offkey, out of tune, outside the lines, or beyond the box, it is all perfect and pure and has the desire to be expressed!

Exact dictation of channeled message:

"Expression is the reason you've all come together in exactly this specific moment. Every single specific moment. Why does a consciousness agree to forget everything it knows, forget who it is, the nature of the universe and of existence? Yes, to remember, to change, to grow, to transform, but ultimately, to express the unique path of transformation and realization it has experienced! The ultimate Joy is the fullest most authentic expression of self in all the resonant ways possible! It is a beautiful thing to experience the process of self-transformation, a beautiful thing. It pales, however, in comparison to the full expression of one's truth in unison with the Universe, who always sings with you. Each expression of your truth, of your true self in whatever way lights you up, is your part of the song of the universe.

Perhaps think of the universe as a giant stage. In a giant theater with amazing acoustics. If no one sings their truth, their song, you can hear the deafening emptiness of the space - almost sad. It just takes one voice to bring life. It takes just one being to sing the song of their soul, to take their stage and shine the light of their song out into the universe, unafraid and unashamed! With each note resounding the beauty and strength of the essence of that soul's journey into the space, the theatre comes alive. The space is full of life, of experience, of joy. Even if the journey was challenging, its expression is always pure joy. And the universe sings back the reflections and harmonies of that journey, the beautiful dialogue of dancing notes, melodies of truth entangling and entwining as they travel through the space! This is with just one voice.

Now, imagine the theatre full of voices singing the exquisite song of their journey into the space. The reflections of joy and Love flowing back to each voice from the universe itself, accepting, embracing, encouraging each voice to sing louder - like a proud parent! Pure Love. Pure Joy. Pure Awe. The Universe can only know itself through us. All of us, in all dimensions. Physical and non-physical. Harmonious and cacophonous. There is only Love.

Our expression is our voice, and our voice is the greatest gift we can give to the universe. The ability to know and experience itself in all the ways possible, devoid of any judgement. When you sing together, no matter what it sounds like, your voices are dancing together in a way that bonds you forever.

My message to you, and all who read these words through your hand is this. Please sing your song, you are why this world exists. You literally are a song from the universe. A song that is never sung is the saddest thing one can experience. Sing your song. Your song is perfect. Your song is beautiful. Your song is the greatest gift you can give. Sing your songs together - hearts with hearts, hands in hands. Dance to the harmonies of the melody of your heart. And when you do, the universe is full of the purest joy and Love. The universe always sings back to you. No voice is ever alone. So, sing your song loud and proud out into the world. And always listen for your response. Be open to all the joy and Love that comes rushing into your life. Listen for the Songs from the Universe in every moment."

Reflections on the channel:

Wow – my truth is a song of the universe. I love that imagery. I can feel what it feels like on that stage with so many mouths closed, with no one singing. That emptiness is what I feel when I don't sing, when I don't express what I need to express! Let us all take Thoth's advice and sing our songs, express our truths!

INTENTION

My intention for you in experiencing these expressions of energy through my lens of poetic words, is that you may PLAY! Throughout my journey, all my trials and tribulations, my path of self-discovery has led me to the following understandings. These are the guidelines I strive to live my life by, every day. And I am honored to have the opportunity to share them with you here. These ideas are not new, but are indeed my version of them through the lens of my personal experience. May you take with you the words that resonate with you, right now, and leave any that do not.

Play is the most sacred act one can do. Play is the expression of joy in the physical world. Play takes the acceptance, love, and mastery of the state of flow that one experiences while in the state of joy, and directs them into the physical world. When one plays, truly plays, there exists no concerns about others' impression or opinion of them, or how they may be judged. They just go, expressing what comes through curiosity and discovery. The playful eyes and heart are more connected to self and all that is, than any others.

Joy is the highest expression of Love, the eternal energy of life. And *play* is the *flow* expression of JOY interacting with the physical world. Thus, my opinion is that PLAY is the highest and most connected expression of life that exists on this planet. When one is engaged in free flow play, they are not experiencing any energetic blockages or limiting beliefs. None of that. It all fades away and all is connected. All time stops, only the present moment matters, their energy shifts and opens in new ways.

PLAY is the great connector. As humans, we are social creatures, we are strongest together. When we are together and functioning coherently in a state of FREE FLOW PLAY, the potential for creativity and healing is massive.

Given this, here is my intention for you and your interactions with the experience of this book.

May you discover more than you expect to.
May you awaken a side of yourself that you've perhaps forgotten or allowed to sleep in the background.
May you sing the words and feel the tones flow through your body, and create internal harmony.
May you illustrate the pages - let your expression of color, line or void, word or not, be the truest and most authentic expression of you in THIS moment.
May this moment BE you, and may you BE this moment.
May any thoughts in your head flow down your neck into your shoulders, through your arm and hands, and onto the page. Making it yours. Making it part of you and your experience in THIS moment.
May the words you read resonate with you at whatever level you need in THIS moment.
May any judgement of self, others, situation, or idea, simply melt out of you through these pages.
May each time you experience any of its aspects be different

and new, as each new sunrise greets us with its unique newness.
May you experience it by yourself and with others.
May you share and reflect.
May this platform show you something about yourself and your world that you weren't aware of.
May your heart open a bit more, as mine did in creating it.
May you allow the wisdom you hold in your bones, cells, and energy to emerge in new ways.
May you revel in the LISTENING to what comes up for you and honoring it.
May whatever path you take lead you to more love, more openness, more JOY.
May you choose LOVE over fear.
May you see time as a tool, not a limitation.
May you embrace the BEAUTY that you are, and that is all around you.
And most of all…
May you PLAY.
May you find creative new ways to experience and express and CREATE the life you want to live.
May you have FUN and BE your glorious self in this beautiful world, TODAY!

INTRODUCTION (WRITTEN IN 2018)

This book is a bit of an accident. I had not intended to write a book of poetry, it just flowed through me. In fact, when I realized it was going to be a book, I had already written 25 of the entries! I had always loved writing and wrote mostly for pleasure to capture my thoughts. Over the past year, I formed the good habit of waking up early and taking an hour or two for myself every morning. I would pour myself a delicious cup of coffee and gaze out my North facing window and just, be. That time was purely mine. I centered myself, set my intention for the day to come, and peacefully welcomed the beautiful Maine morning.

I also started writing during my morning meditations. At first, I wrote my thoughts, feelings, aspirations, to-do lists and the like. Then all of a sudden, my thoughts landed on the page in melody, in verse, and with vividly painted images and tones. I don't remember the exact day that my morning writings changed, but I do know that once the poems and stories started coming, they didn't stop!

Each one, each morning, was truly an experience for me. As I mentioned, I saw the most vivid of images and the words sang in my head. The words danced along the page as they danced through my head. Each word, sentence, idea and image, carrying with it a corresponding tone. It was truly mesmerizing. I was completely absorbed in the experience, the sounds, the images, that I utterly lost track of time, space, and who I was. I was one with the experience of creation, and it was beautiful.

The intoxicating start to my day always left me feeling light, grateful and fully satisfied. I felt full and whole in a way I hadn't felt before. Each morning the experience grew more and more vivid, and more and more beautiful. The topics hit closer and closer to home for me as I felt myself changing, opening up to new experiences, and to a new way of being.

My brain was changing, I could feel it. My experiences were changing, everything in my life felt more manageable. I had more capacity to deal with everyday events in a calm and centered way. I was in 'Flow'. The more I experienced this, the better and lighter and more capable I felt.

This book is an attempt to offer you the experience of my morning meditations, to give you the fullest opportunity possible to explore through your various senses, the path I took over the past year. I hope you enjoy and explore through color, sound, the written word, and anything else you dream up, the pages to come. I would love to hear from you about your experiences with this book and how you notice yourself change!

THE STATE OF FLOW

The state of flow is a beautiful thing to experience. First discovered and named by Hungarian psychologist, Mihaly Csikszentmihalyi, flow is a state of externally focused attention. When we are in flow, we become one with the activity we are doing. If we are painting, we become the act of painting. If playing music, we become the act of playing music. Running long distances, we are no longer the runner, we are the act of running. In this state, it is impossible to worry about bills, what people will think of you, or anything else that may be taking up valuable brain space in our everyday lives. Csikszentmihalyi describes the experience of flow as:

1. Being completely involved in what you are doing – focused, concentrated
2. Having a sense of ecstasy of being outside everyday reality
3. Having great inner clarity – knowing what needs to be done, and how well we are doing
4. Knowing that the activity is doable and that our skills are adequate to the task

5. A sense of serenity – no worries about oneself, and a feeling of growing beyond the boundaries of the ego
6. Timelessness – thoroughly focused on the present, hours seem to pass in minutes
7. Intrinsic motivation – whatever produces flow becomes its own reward[1]

Our brains can only process so much information at any given time. When we are experiencing flow states, we use all our available brain 'bandwidth' for the activity we are flowing with. We don't have extra brain capacity to worry about whatever was on our minds before we started the activity, our worries or concerns, or to even sense that we exist.

We go in and out of focused states all day long, focusing on different things, more or less intently depending on what our brain deems important for our survival. These states of focused attention can range from paying attention in class (external focus), to internal focus when we ruminate on our daily worries. When in flow, we give our brains' a break from emotional stress – this gives our bodies a break from the stress hormones (mostly cortisol and adrenaline) that bombard our system when we experience stress – these can ultimately cause physical damage to our bodies if we are under constant stress.

According to Positive Psychology, "In flow, our brain waves shift from the beta waves of concentration to the alpha waves associated with rest and relaxation and the theta waves that occur during meditation."[2]

According to Psychology Today regarding a 2011 study, "Even with this small amount of practice (a study averaging

[1] https://www.ted.com/talks/mihaly_csikszentmihalyi_on_flow/up-next

[2] https://positivepsychlopedia.com/year-of-happy/benefits-of-flow/

5 hours and 16 minutes of meditation training per participant), the researchers found big differences in brain functioning. Specifically, meditation training seemed to shift activity in the frontal regions of the brain towards a pattern indicative of greater positive, approach-oriented emotional states."[3] By incorporating these alpha and theta brain waves into our lives, we can physically change our brains.

[3] https://www.psychologytoday.com/intl/blog/choke/201110/meditation-small-dose-big-effect

HOW TO USE THIS

Use this book however your heart desires! I offer you as many methods of sensory participation as I can in this format. Please feel free to mix and match in a way that works for you, helps you find peace and flow, and really any kind of enjoyment.

Here are some suggestions:

1. Read the words on the page in your head while humming whatever melody comes into your head spontaneously
2. Find something to color with (crayons, pencils, paints, markers… anything) and illustrate the book YOUR way
3. Read an entry, find stillness for a moment, allow the energy of the entry to flow through you and allow it to move your body in whatever way is right for you – dance, jump, run, stretch, anything!
4. Each time you read one of the 33 entries, add more to your illustration, more color, more drawings…

6. After you add some color to an entry, hand it to someone you love to add some color of their own

7. Get a group of your favorite people together and all read on entry together and illustrate your own, then discuss the experience with each other

8. If you have a fight with someone, both sit together and read an entry aloud and illustrate it, then talk about your experience doing that together

9. If your kids can't settle down to do their homework or get to sleep – read or sing them an entry, illustrate it with them, then tell them how much you love them and continue on to sleep or homework

As you see, there are infinite applications for this experience. I look forward to hearing more creative ways to use it that you discover!

THE PLAY

1 Golden Threads

In one moment,
I saw the golden threads of creation and knew that I was sewn by them.
I felt the wind of time,
and I knew that breath filled my lungs.
I basked in the warmth of love
and I knew it was the same love that filled my heart.
I witnessed the light of a sea of souls,
and knew mine was among them.
The same Light in the tree
was the light in me.
The same wind bellowing in the lungs of all,
is the same that breaths in me.

2 Becoming Me

Kali, beloved Kali
I surrender to you my fear of men,
for I trust you with my fear.
I surrender my anxiety to you,
for I trust you with my anxiety.
I surrender to you all my insecurities,
for I trust you with my true self.
I surrender to you my pain and suffering,
for I trust you with my soul, my body.
I surrender to you my fear of failure,
for I trust you with my path, my purpose.
I surrender my shame to you,
for I trust you with my truth.
I surrender to you my pride, my ego,
for I trust you with my soul.
I surrender to you my self-judgement,
for I trust you with myself.
I surrender to you my judgement of others,
for I trust you with my life.
I surrender to you my doubt,
for I trust you with my truth.
As I let go and step away
from all that no longer serves me,
I pass my reflection and through the ash
I see myself clearly for the first time.

3 Dance

As I wake and greet the day,
I thank all who are with me, in love,
for my highest and greatest good,
and the highest and greatest good of all.
My gratitude is bottomless,
for it wells up from the deep void of my soul,
my creation, my knowing.
All that I desire already exists in my darkness,
my shadow, my womb.
As I bless each beautiful aspect of my being,
my past, my present, my future,
all energies of growth and transition.
I watch the ever-continuous
dance of transformation ebb and flow,
with the certainty of tides.
I bless the dance!
I bless the NOT knowing my next partner,
or next steps, or where I'll land
I bless the thrill!
I bless the Joy and Wonder!
I dive deep into the beautiful velvet Darkness,
this sacred time to know myself,
to remember.
As I cry tears of joy and sorrow,
reminiscing,
I match the footsteps of dances gone by.
The steps I remember,
the partners I know all too well.
Some will live forever in my heart,
reminding me who I am
and where I'm going.
While others I bid farewell,
as we trace our footsteps one last time.
My truth of now only existing for an instant,

rising through flames into being,
only to plummet back into the darkness
and reunite with itself.
Reveling in the silent symphony of the Dark Mother,
the stillness of rejuvenation,
and the thick dark fullness of potential.
I embrace these moments of full oneness,
of knowing,
of grounded stability,
for through these moments
I know myself.
It is only through this knowing that I can trust.
And trust I do.
I trust the darkness to embrace the Light
in balanced perfection.
I trust my soul to guide me with its wisdom.
I trust my body to know the steps
to the song it's not yet heard.
I trust my heart to feel in perfect timing,
in resonance with the Dark Mother herself,
and with all that is.
And as the orchestra tunes itself to a tone only she can hear,
I hear the words… "care to dance?"

4 Story of a Moment

The morning is thick,
I feel it press against my face as I step fearlessly and gratefully into the day.
Time, expiring slowly,
is replenishing my soul moment by moment.
With the death of each moment,
the birth of the next draws me in.
I stand here,
rooted in time and space while soaring seamlessly through the ages.
Time Stops.
This is the moment I've been waiting for.
Searching the globe for this exact moment for lifetimes, it seems.
Heartbeats slow, breathing stops, thinking wanes.
My attempt to fully BE this particular moment
I want to BE THIS MOMENT!
Its timeless beauty and wonder.
Its essence pure and joyful,
yet still and empty.
Full of Emptiness.
The world continues without me,
while I linger,
drawing my moment into myself.
I take it in fully and embrace it,
inviting it into all of me,
each cell, each thought, each feeling.
Infusing all of me with the one perfect moment
I've waited an eternity for.
I draw it down into my core,
through my feet,
into the earth all the way to her core.
We journey together in this stillness we've created,
to just be together a bit longer.

I sit in stillness with my new companion,
down in my core, our core,
enveloped by the black silk of newness,
of potential.
I know my time here is running out and I must return
to the ticking clock of time.
Seeds of sadness begin to sprout with the realization,
and I begin to detach from my new friend
and rise from the Darkness.
In the moments of our Journey back to the world,
she shared with me her secret…
"I am the essence of all moments, not just one.
My place is deep in the heart of every instant!
I wait patiently to be discovered,
over and over again,
by you and all who are.
By seeing me, you give me life.
By sitting with me you give me purpose.
By loving me, you love yourself, and I am free!
I hope to see you and sit with you again,
in every moment.
Seek me out,
for I sit patiently waiting
to feel your gaze upon me once more."
I find my body and take a breath,
finally ready to see.

5 Trust

When time stops flowing and all is unstuck,
we reverberate between the seams.
Expressing what could be or what wasn't,
on an imagined timeline we created.
Release.
A challenging act.
An action of
Inaction.
Acceptance of what IS,
cannot come until we SEE
what is.
Delusions rampant cloud our sight,
and we hardly see the shadows.
The outlines fragmented and disjointed among the ash,
the smoke, the mist.
It's a challenge to even see ourselves clearly anymore.
Where one stops and the next begins,
questionable.
We drudge along searching for meaning, answers,
a key to the language of Life.
A foreign tongue we've not heard before
At least, we don't remember hearing it.
Its roots remain, while branches dwindle,
unseen by our human form.
A leaf appears!
A shining glimmer of Light,
of Hope.
It speaks of other leaves,
many more just like it,
holding wisdom and Light,
and Hope.
The tales of branches must be true,
for I've seen the leaves they hold.
Their stories passed down,

tales unseen,
of glorious trees with branches full,
they bear the fruit of wonder.
Wholeness.
Truth.
I know they exist,
I've seen the signs.
I trust.
I trust.
I trust.

6 I AM

I am here, I am now.
I am as much as I am, and I'm simply not what I'm not.
I am the Light, I am the Dark.
I am that tiny wonderous spark.
I am the rocks, I am the trees.
I am the water flowing through the seas.
I am the protector of all beings.
I see the light in everything.
I am the soul to rise above,
I live inside of every hug.
I am the connector of all things.
I cherish you, and me, and we.
In times of Darkness, I make the space for growth and timeless yearning.
I am the action to and fro.
I am the stillness down below.
I am the Earth, I am the seas.
I am the waking of the trees.
I am a being of Light and Love.
I've come to serve you from above.
I'm every step in every journey.
I am the tears and Joy of learning
I am the path you're on today.
I'm with you each and every day.
I am the master, I am the teacher,
Pushing you to reach in deeper.
I am the pain, I am the strife,
I cut your ego with a knife.
I blow down trees, I bring new sprouts.
I am the wind that carries you home.
I am the error, I am the treason.
I am the changing of the season.
I am the clouds, striated, glowing,
From beneath them, I'm the knowing.

I learn from you, you help me grow.
I am the time that helps me know.
I help you make some room to cry.
I'm here with you from days gone by.
I am the rock, the solid foundation,
That turns to sand with incantation.
I am the turning of the tides.
I am the memories in your eyes.
I am the painted window pane,
Peeled from sun and years of strain.
I am the shedding, the letting go.
I am the new, I am the old.
The tried and true, the never told.
I am the waiting, I am the depts.
I am the tangled, knotted web.
I am the mirror, I am the lens.
I am the pilgrim, turning heads.
I'm timeless beauty in us all.
I catch you gently when you fall.
When time is done, and all is still,
I am the Love, the Joy, the Thrill.
Along this journey, short and sweet,
I am the YOU, you've yet to meet.

7 Search

As the days shift,
the seasons change,
Time continues,
and I am still.
With layers obscured,
I forge ahead,
Continuing the search…

8 Process

I am human, watch me err.
I've hurt someone I love.
With ego large, I'm short to see.
The beauty that's in front of me.
Seeing flow from eyes of rigidity,
missed the journey down the river.
Needing to direct and control the flow of things,
Denies the ever-constant transformation.
The beauty, the experience, the mystery, all die.
The rigid cube does not flow,
nor does it fit.
The gaps between its edges and the undefinable shoreline, match the gaps of consciousness.
I failed to see the worth,
I couldn't see the beauty there in front of me.
She was the flow,
the river,
she was undefinable, uncontainable.
She was the opposite of me.
I was the box with straight and pointy edges.
I float along down the river, ignoring the flow beneath me.
If only the river had straight shores and flat bottom, measurable and containable.
Think how fast the water would flow without disturbances,
I mused.
Think how we wouldn't have anything to fear,
for the flow would be contained.
We'd know its contents, its shape, its limits.
No more fear of the unknown, for all would be known.
Knowing the past, present and future,
I'll know what to do, how to prepare, everything.
I'll be safe, I'll know no lack, no defeat.
Always in control.
Always safe.

Nothing to fear.
Nothing new,
no surprise,
no spontaneity,
no excitement.
The smallest and most intricate creatures,
spaces, experiences, interactions…
All live in the spaces between, where things meet.
Intersections, the birthplace of beauty and the glorious new.
The fractal-like infinity between the tiny meeting the tiny in spaces unknown.
It all dies in a box.
Try to contain the river in a box,
it stops flowing.
It is no longer a river.
Stripped of its beauty and wonder,
it ceases to be
The river is gone.
The flow is gone.
The life is gone.
Everything dies in a box.
Isolated, constricted, out of context.
Nothing exists in a box, devoid of meaning, devoid of self.
All life dies.
I begin to wake up to the truth that I too am the river.
Pretending to be a box.
I deny my nature, my truth, my self.
I cease to be.
Watching the flow threatens my straight sides.
How does a 'box' become the river?
I separate my hard straight sides,
Disintegrated corners,
and one by one they jump into the river.
Taken by the current,
Allowing the wonder of the unknown tomorrow to return!

9 Grounded

The grounding in, I feel it deep inside my inner sanctum.
The twitching torment steps aside,
It's not its time or moment.
The time is now to reach in deep and find the inner beauty.
The strength and power coursing through to every cell inside me.
From selves gone by, I'm hypnotized,
I've come to break the cycle.
When veils of judgement cloak the truth,
we can't become our splendor.
We watch it glimmer far away,
With hopes to someday meet it.
With veils of gray atop our frowns,
Embedded in the layers,
We cannot know our splendor yet.
She's hidden from our senses.
When gray prevails, no color lives.
Consuming all that sparkles.
What color is your splendor now?
Can you even remember?
The blue of skies?
The green of trees?
Yellow of sundrenched flowers?
Whichever one, or maybe few,
Though many years estranged.
Invite her in, to share some tea,
A cozy reuniting.
For when she's close, inside your heart
She lights your inner sanctum.
She shows you colors 'twix the veils,
Colors from years forgotten.
Its time, perhaps, to set her free.
Into the world to glimmer.
But not before you share with her

Your silky velvet shadow.
For cloaked in this, your grounding deep,
She finds her saturation.
Clutching the deep and endless void,
The darkness of creation.
Your splendor now,
Can plant the seeds,
For future generations.
Instead of soaring through the sky,
Not touching down or rooting.
She now can sit upon the earth,
And feel her every movement.
She plants her seeds,
All cloaked by darkest velvet.
To bear the seeds of color bright,
With roots of saturation.
The lightness of the Splendor's seeds,
Could 'ner before take hold here.
With weighted cloaks of darkness voids,
Envelops sparkling sunshine.
The Splendor's seeds of colors bright,
Can now take hold and blossom.
Allowing sprouts of colors new,
To carpet all the planet.
With roots down deep,
We all can reap,
New shades of peace and glory.
When colors abound, no gray is found.
It's judgement's day to dwindle.

10 My Truth

I sing my truth, I hear it ring,
It resonates inside me!
I know my truth, I sing it clear
From deep inside my guarded lair.
It breathes new life into my bones,
They're stronger than I've ever known.
I feel my truth inside my core,
It touches every part of me.
It is that light from deep within,
It powers every movement.
Each choice, each word, with loving sword
I cut facades right open.
I speak my truth, no lies you'll see,
Shoot out from every part of me.
With brilliant rays of golden sun,
Disinfecting everyone.
We cannot change what we don't see.
I'll show you what's in front of thee.
Divine compassion wrapped in gold,
Are worthless if they're never told.
I'm here to be, to set it free,
The truth that sits inside of me.
My truth is power, strength and love
As if from guiding hands above.
From depths below, I find the strength to outwardly embody
The truth I know and feel so deep.
My power that's inside of me.
My truth must be, it must exist,
If not, I'm rendered powerless.
With languished truth, my soul dies too
The part of me that cannot be.
It's for this reason I must do
What may seem mean or harsh or rude.
For when I speak my truth out loud,

Be it alone or in a crowd.
My power grows, from head to toes,
It sings inside my every prose.
I'm here, my dear, to break on through,
With words that cut the false in two.
The golden brilliance rises new.
To shower out upon the world.
The change of hope, becomes the new,
To shed all that you find askew.
Without your power, light and truth,
Your words fall flat, your actions cold.
Without the truth to help it hold,
The empty words collapse with doubt.
They wither down upon the day,
And disappear in puffs of gray.
My truth, I sing it loud and clear,
For all to hear it, far and near.
I have no shame, no sorrow, no heaviness,
Around the truth I speak.
The truth transforms you once it's in,
It knocks down every door.
It's up to you, your soul, your root,
Whether or not you answer.
She'll sweep you off your feet, it's true,
To show you what's in front of you.
She makes no judgement through and through,
She'll sit there waiting patiently, out there upon your doorstep.
Be it in this life or the next,
she sits, in Love, to help you shed.
The story of my truth's not done,
it's a story that has just begun.
For when she knocks upon your door,
invite your truth to greet her.
When they lock eyes, you'll realize,
All truths untold are Love.

11 This Morning's Teacher

My heart is full, the day is crisp,
And full of expectations.
I stand here at my window's edge,
to breath, to stop, to focus.
What's real to me, this wonderous day,
the flow of life unfolding.
Revealing more each coming day,
Of me, of time, of loving.
I watch the morning, crisp and new,
From my enchanted window.
It shows me what I need to see,
Reflecting every bit to me.
Each tone, each shade, each sparkle, each shadow.
Each one a brand new teacher.
With lessons fair, and gifts to bear,
Each one in time shows beauty.
The snow atop each roof and branch,
Upon the streets and sidewalks.
Reminds me clear, to focus near,
To turn inside and settle.
I settle in and look within,
To find each shade's reflection.
What do they show me inside ME?
The world is but a mirror.
It shows me things that I hold dear,
The times I feel the brightest.
I wrap them up inside my soul,
To study every corner.
Their imprint stays, feelings remain,
And then in time release them.
This liberation cycles through,
With each a little freer.
The next time there's reflections here.
I'll see a little deeper.

Into the cavern of my being,
reflecting my new teacher.
I walk this path into my cave,
of twists and turns and trials.
Each step towards self discovery,
The prize I seek,
is ME!

12 You

When moments stop, when hearts connect.
That's where you'll find me waiting.
Where love pulls through, where puppies play,
That's where I'll be, just smiling.
As birds soar high above the trees,
As pedestrians struggle through the sleet,
As sea lions bask and wait for heat,
That's where you'll find me.
Inside a cozy cup of tea,
Inside a laugh with two or three,
Inside the roots of every tree,
That is where I'll be
Embedded in each helping hand,
Entangled with each loving look,
Entrenched in every word of truth,
That's where you'll find me.
Each frost of winter,
Each bird of spring,
Each sunny summers day,
Each autumn wind, holds me within,
Each hug, each kiss, each tale of sin,
Each look of admiration.
The stillest pond, the roughest sea,
That's where you'll find me.
Each tear of sorrow, each warm embrace,
Each lesson learned, each victory's taste,
That's where you'll find me.
I am the essence of all things,
From here and through the cosmos.
Throughout all time, you too can find,
Me in all things just waiting.
I am the love inside all things,
Awaiting activation.
The only thing I'm waiting for,

The only thing I need.
For you to find me, set me free.
Search for me in every moment.
All that's required, for love to BE,
The final piece… is you!

13 My Song

I come inside, in from the tide,
Beneath its jagged surface.
The beaks and valleys hide the truth,
Embedded in the mountain.
I know all answers that I need,
Are here inside my bones.
All I've to do is listen through,
To all that's being said.
They speak to me with every breath,
With every movement, with every touch.
I hear them tell me things I know,
In every situation.
The truth they sing,
My bones they ring.
In vibratory concert.
My challenge here,
To keep faith near,
Inspecting every corner.
To reunite my thoughts and heart,
Bring my whole being together.
To learn the language of my bones,
My heart, my soul, my person.
Is to sing my song of truth,
The song I've always known.
The melody I've heard before,
The words are now familiar.
For so long now,
Exist alone, in separate isolation.
Third thing it needs, is one to sing,
The words and tune together.
The song of me, it cannot be,
Without these three ingredients.
For words alone, make no one dance,
And just a tune lacks meaning.

Neither can be,
Without the ME,
to stitch the two together.
When words meet notes,
A song is born,
Let's sing our own together.
In blessed joy we harmonize
And rise above together!

14 Confluence

As we sail along together,
The magic swirls about.
Golden eddies of transformation and discovery.
We sail on the same sea.
While our attempts to separate
the oceans and the seas.
The lines we draw disintegrate,
The separations blur.
The time has come to realize
Without sword and without bow,
The lines we draw for protection,
Aren't part of me or you.
When we can look beyond these lines,
And truly integrate
Our souls, and lives, and laughs, and cries,
Become the only focus.
For when we truly are at peace,
With everyone inside us
The confluence reverberates,
The flow in me and you.

15 Our Path

By meeting others on my path,
I see myself in them.
The things I know, the things I fear,
The things that I hold dear.
While everyone I meet and know
Is on their own path now.
We find the more we look and see,
That their own path is mine.
They walk my path and I walk theirs,
We share this road together.
We forge each step, try not to fall,
We trial, and we worry.
We isolate and squelch the love
That binds our paths together.
For lack of sight we choose to fight
Instead of work together.
We all have but one common goal,
To love and to be loved.
With sword and shield we separate
Our lives from one another.
The ever binding glue of eternal love,
That we all are
Remains whether we choose to see or not.
The glue that binds the roads we walk
Is love, love, love.
This love doesn't ask where you're going,
It asks not where you're from.
It doesn't care the clothes you wear
Or where your degree is from.
It doesn't care mistakes you made,
For each one was a lesson.
A brilliant bead to plant a seed
For love inside each action.
Each moment of stillness each busy day,

Each hurt, each breath, each moment.
We wrap our wings around each heart,
The golden wings of feathered light,
The brilliance and the joy.
To all who hurt me through my life,
I send you love and blessings.
To those who felt the need to fight,
I send you peace and calm.
To those who hold to negativity
For any person, place, or instance,
I send to you the color blue –
Release, renew, let go.
My prayer to Love and all that is,
For these two are the same,
Is for the help to see what's true,
Inside of me and you.
For you are me with different care,
with different eyes and ears.
The roles we play from day to day,
Obscure sometimes our purpose.
To see ourselves in me and you.
To honor and to value.
Each role we take the time to make,
To see a new perspective.
Will show us what we've yet to learn,
By staying with our fears.
Invite them in from days gone by,
There's truth in every moment.
With loving touch, all wrapped with hope
For a bright new tomorrow.
To raise a glass and thank the light
and the sustaining darkness.
For each opportunity to see
Another side of me.
Since I am you and you are me,
The dogs we feed are different.

We might take slightly different steps
In any given moment.
But the path we're on is one,
The only road is love.

16 Nature Speaks

In a time when nature speaks,
Through each of our eyes.
Each step I take,
each barrier we break,
Will close the gap for love.
The stillest water all around,
Brings peace to every fiber.
The give and take,
The to and fro,
Exchanging Love forever.
The depts of old,
Entrenched and cold,
Warm every bit inside me.
With truth and glee, reality,
Envelopes all my thinking.
I am the sea, and the sea is me.
We love the world together.

17 The Fog

With foggy skies and joyful eyes,
The water content rises.
Absorbed, abundant through the air,
To cleanse each part of me.
Each breath drawn in brings love within,
Transitions' transformation.
Beloved stones, the cult unknown,
Brings beauty deep within.
With blinking once, two times, a third,
We marvel at each moment.
The grateful tone lies far below,
Any construct or misguidance.
It's here to show me,
It has arrived, beguiled and bewildered.
From stones within, brings crystals in
Into my darkest knowing.
The fog, it brings its density,
I feel its heavy presence.
Reflecting mirrors in each spec,
To show me inside secrets.
The tiny mirrors show me deep
Into my very soul.
What lies in there, it's time to share,
The aspirations, old.
What song I yearn to sing so loud,
To shout it from the rooftops.
The song emerging from my soul.
Each day I see,
Each note is me,
My journey inside deepens.
Each tiny note, a mirror of the fog,
Reminds me deeper.
Of who I am and why I'm here.
Of what I have to share.

It's endless, what I have to give,
An endless, joyous, cycle.
Of love and joy,
Of compassion and growth,
Reflections of my soul.
I thank the fog for showing me,
With tiny mirrored droplets,
In every breath, in every step.
What's deep inside of me.
The water heals, I am the sea,
With waves of physicality.
Water and light and music's tone,
That's all we've come to be.
The elements comprising
Our foundation deep and strong,
For LOVE inside us all.
Water is the love we feel
In us and all around us.
Light is the sparkle that we feel
Illuminates us all.
Music is the song we sing
Through each and every action.
It brings to life,
Invites to dance,
With every lighted droplet.
For once you start to sing your song,
Allow your own vibrations.
The ripples of your song will ring,
Through all that it encounters.
So, sing your song,
Sing loud and clear,
Through each and every moment.
And thank the fog for showing you
How beautiful you are.

18 Peaceful Warrior

The churning taurus of light and love,
Of color and of tone.
I feel it's swirling flow of life,
Around me every second.
The leaning forward, turning in,
Cyclical journeys of truth.
Returns to what we know so true,
In spite of constant fear.
When rattled, shaken, strewn about,
Return to flow and moment.
For it is being, flow, and now
That brings us back to center.
That center point inside your gut
The one you can't ignore.
It shows you when each cycle ends,
Another one begins.
No termination, just evolution,
A spiraled swirl of you.
For breathing in and breathing out
Creates this tender cycle.
Follow your breath to know yourself,
From every lovely angle.
I breath in all my energy
I've sent out to the world.
All parts of me I've left behind,
I summon back to me now.
All cleared and centered,
Bright and true,
Sheds all that is not you.
Returning back, those bits of me,
With joy and love for journey.
I breath in also nature's gifts,
From trees, from rocks, from seas.
The salted air with sea gulls' cries,

Cleanses me in and out.
The ambient love that makes the world,
I breath all that in too.
The solid, grounding, love from all
The deepest darkest oceans.
They send to me the nurtured depths,
From humpback whales to mermaids,
From Kali's velvet swirling womb,
Through molten flowing lava.
Through layers, life and density,
Exploring radiant truths.
Through darkest depths under the sea,
Down, down below light's reaches.
An underworld of mystery,
Of hope, of love, of me.
I breath in all velvety depths,
Reflecting in my corners
Through all the layers, ocean depths,
Residing with their beauty.
I breathe all of that wisdom in,
With each and every breath.
I breathe it through my toes to head,
Up through my golden Hara.
Straight through the sky,
The clouds up high,
To soar with heaven's bodies.
Through the moon, which shows me now,
Exactly who I am.
Reflecting every bit of me,
For all of life to see!
It's proud reflection, showing bright,
The song we each do sing.
For when we all gaze at her face,
We hear our song inside.
I breath through, this harmony,
And share it far beyond.

The song is sung all through the sky,
And permeates the ages.
Love's beacon here,
For us to share, with every living creature.
And as I breathe in all that is,
With timeless love and gratitude,
I'm bigger with each breath.
I'm stronger, backed by all that is,
I cannot be ignored.
My power in each moment is
An open loving door.
My power comes from only Love,
Life's one connecting force.
I am the Peaceful Warrior.
I love. I love. I love.

19 Glowing Embers

As glowing embers light the landscape on this blue gray morning.
The softest hues paint purples and blues as peaceful wisps crossing the sky.

Pedestrians stroll through slick and ice to reach their destinations.
They crunch through slush encased with ice, they breath in this new day.

Just poking through the ice and snow, are brand new signs of life.
With roots so deep inside the Earth, they draw from every being.

And Kali sings to help me see the depths of what she brings.
Then Lakshmi takes my hand in hers and guides me to the surface.
To see what now can come to be, we hold it in our hearts.
Like pure white light passing through a prism here on Earth.
With transformation's colors spew about to every surface!

What brilliance comes into your view, when seeing through these colors?
The endless bounty overflows into the hearts of many.

Connecting heaven and the depths, creating Life a plenty
All colors, shapes, sizes and hues, each one a little different.

The most potent beauty of all, comes when we play together.
Our many hands can reach as one, to stroke the growing lotus.
And when it blooms, our hearts consume, the light from one another.

20 Light and Dirt

As the brilliant sun does rise, so does my day
The crispness of the snowy morning tickles my face with a slight breeze
I feel the ocean, I feel the seas.
Welling up inside me from the depths of my soul.
What may it bring?
What glorious gifts might the oceans and the seas bring me on this glorious morning?
Truth?
Home?
Light?
All the gifts of Gaia come to me, bounding towards me with open arms and beautiful love to share.
We are the world
We are your world
And you are part of it.
You are the oceans and the seas.
Know them, for they make you whole.
Greet them, for they will set you free.
Know who you are and where you come from.
They sky is part of the ocean.
The ocean a dense sky.
There is only difference in experience of each.
You are the sun.
The sun's light touches her sweet Earth,
And life is born of light and dirt.
Face that sun head on, show your light to her.
Reflecting each other's brilliance.
She wants to see you.
For in you she sees herself.
You are the Moon.
Honor her brilliance and reflect her light back for her to see.
For then does she know herself.
Through you and your reflection of luminous light.

Show her your inside and she will show you hers
Show your beautiful light in all that you do, to everyone you meet.
For then will you know yourself a bit more and rejoice in your splendor, and that of all.

21 The New Us

I now let go of all I think,
Of all I thought I knew
To be right now, fully engaged
With who I want to be.
For who I am, this moment now,
Today and every day
Constantly gone, forever changed,
With my next breath, I'm new.
This being that I am right now
Is special and unique
I will never be her again
I'll never have this moment
Or chance to walk this path
Inside this self again
And as she fades into the world
Becoming sky and ocean
She reunites with brilliant night
With trees and rocks and flowers
For she, along with all past 'me's
And 'you's and 'he's and 'she's
Create this world we know today
They share our every moment.
Let's send them love as we're reborn
In every single moment.
Let's thank them for the time we've had
And every lesson learned
Each thought, each care,
Each vista shared,
Imprints on our past person.
Now let them be,
To set you free,
To be the NEW today.
While I stand here and write these words
With every of my fibers,

I gaze out my window to the bay
Atop the trees and buildings
I've looked out this window many times,
And every time it's different
Today's blue water never seen,
Reflecting bluest skies
With sunlight rays illuminating
All they see right now
As shadows shift
New sights emerge
A gift to this new NOW
Embrace it all, each new delight,
A treat for each NEW person
When we emerge and then take flight
From all the love around us
We rise like phoenix from the ash
And a whole new world is born.

22 I Choose Peace

I woke inside a snow globe
The silent swirling of joyful bits of life
Of snow, of water, of energy.
Of I AM
I gaze into it, into the chaos with peace
I AM part of it.
I feel one with the chaos and the peace
For it is only through chaos that I can know peace
The contrast shows truth
I am always presented with a choice to be of one or the other
In any given situation
NOW
I CHOOSE PEACE.

23 Leave Our Mark

Connection, the tool of evolution.
Method of our interconnectedness
Heart, the tool of connection.
When we see ourselves in love,
We can too see all things in that same love
All beings

Shine, the tool of heart.
For only when we shine can we see the love.
Only when we allow ourselves to shine,
Can we see others shine.
Only when we see others shine,
Can we love them,
Wholly and truly.

Mark, the tool of shine.
When we allow ourselves to mark the world
And ourselves with love
We leave traces of that love.
Like trails for others to follow.
We leave trails of Love tracing our trajectory through time and space

Let our Mark be love.
Yet each mark IS love
Be it the potential, the manifestation
The cry for it, a reach, a gift of it.
We are all love, wholly and fully.
The warm peachy pink of the beautiful sky
This wonderous morning shows me just that
As it warms my heart, leaving its mark,
I thank GAIA, all that is, all that has been, and all that will be.
For we are on the path to discovering the love we are

Learning how to share that love with each other
And the world around us

May our connections be strong
May our hearts burst with unconditional Love and Joy
And may our Marks be the fullest expression of love and joy
That we can experience
In any given moment.

24 Time

Another day begins, time slows, every breath fills my body as it does yours.
Time is a funny thing, although not really a thing at all.
Time is a story we tell ourselves.
We teach time, and time in turn teaches us.
What do we really know to be true?
Who are we really, that we need the stories?
The varied path of self discovery is winding indeed, and beautiful.
For at times we are given gifts of 2 or 3.
Three, the trinity is powerful indeed.
Three sides create a triangle,
The shape that forms the spiral,
Inside it harnesses and perpetuates the constant flow of life energy.
Never stopping, always growing.
With depths unknown, and heights yet untouched by your experience.
You know it to be the most basic structure of things, of ideas, of everything.
Our souls travel though time in threes,
We perpetuate ourselves, our paths, our missions, and our essences.
Because of the multi-faceted nature of our beings, our energy
We can be, and usually are, part of many trinities.
Sometimes they manifest all in one life, sometimes not, they may skip several lives.
As they weave through space, dimension, and time,
Their force propels us forward,
And sometimes simultaneously backward,
Time is tricky
Whether we know about it or not.
The force is always felt, but many times not identified.
When a trinity becomes aware of itself,

When its elements align in consciousness,
True power is possible.
Wielding the spiraled force of the trinity is a love that is undeniable and beautiful.

Trees in threes
Skies of blue
Aim for love
Tried and true
Once a line
Now a spiral
Ever flowing
Ever true
Embrace a branch
Hold its bark
Feel the roots
Know the spark
Then with angels
Holding hands
Find a truth
That holds the plan

25 Haze

On the fall of things,
Takes up in two.
My foot is fallen,
And so, have you.
The time entrenched is but a trine,
Moving faster in your mind.
The way is called upon it's true,
It's come from me, and me to you.
In time we trust
Each other's ways,
When fighting through,
We see the haze.
I trail about with common thought.
Allowing nothing be for naught.
And through these days of twisted lies.
You've come to know, and trust your eyes.
What lies beneath, through eyes we seek,
You've captured all mountains and peaks.
For we are one,
My sister dear,
The one is told
With child near.
For time will hold,
What time will bear.

26 Mists of Creation

This is a story of a woman, seemingly in peril.
"Oh, woe is me," she proclaims
As her words wrap around her,
Constricting her tighter.
"What shall become of me?"
There is nothing on her horizon,
For her words have blinded her.
They are so thick with the density of her mind.
And the thicker her words,
The less she saw.
One day, this woman had a memory pop into her awareness.
A memory of long ago,
In days gone by.
But she couldn't place it.
She was there,
For sure, but as what?
She did not know.
She must have been there,
For she had this vivid memory of it.
Fogs and mists among the leafed branches.
Flowers, creaks, and rocks.
Trees a plenty,
She sees it all,
But what was she?
At first, she thought,
"Perhaps I'm a bird sitting in a tree branch,"
And so immediately upon that thought appearing,
She found her memory soar into the branches of the nearest tree!
It was as if she was magically transformed into the idea she just had!
Then she thought,
"Well, if I'm a bird, I can surely fly. Let me fly above the tree tops and see the Earth

From the beautiful sky!"
And so, it was.
Her awareness took flight
And she was off,
Into the misty morning,
Gazing down at the treetops, amazed.
After a few minutes of soaring about,
Feeling the warm morning breeze sift between her feathers,
The thought…
"Now, how amazing would it be if I were an insect,
Able to burrow down into the earth
Among the leafy, peaty forest floor!"
And immediately upon thinking this thought,
She was immersed in leaves,
Gigantic leaves decomposing all around her.
The rich energy from the Earth was all around her
Tiny hard body.
And she dug and dug,
Unearthing many tasty bits and microbes
Which she immediately ate with joy and delight!
She never in a million years thought she would find
SO MUCH JOY in eating tiny soil dwellers,
But she was.
She was in pure bliss,
Fully aligned with her little buggy purpose.
How simple it all was,
And how joyful!
She reveled in the simplicity for awhile
Until she 'remembered' she was only in a memory…
But of what?
What was this magical place where your thoughts
Became 'real' only upon thinking them,
And anything was possible?
It seemed so real.
But, "it can't be real.
I've not seen or heard of anything like this before."

And immediately upon thinking that,
She was back home,
Tied up in her words,
Bound by her thoughts and feelings,
And unfortunate beliefs.
"Oh, woe is me!
It was all a dream!
I am bound by my words and thoughts forever!"
And the words tied about her got tighter
And tighter.
After such a beautiful and liberating dream,
Her condition seemed even more
Unbearable.
She had felt freedom!
She had felt empowerment!
Her thoughts created beautiful experiences
In that magical place!
Oh, how could she get there again?
Could she?
And while she was in the midst of feeling
Especially sorry for herself,
She had a thought…
"Wait, in that magical place,
My thoughts made my experiences.
Was that the key?
But I have all these words around me!
They're so tight!"
She wondered if the magical rules could help her here.
And as she wondered,
She gazed out her little window
And saw a bird and an insect
Standing on her window sill
Just staring at her.
As if waiting for her to realize something.
As she watched them,
Still, and looking directly at her,

She wondered…
"Those can't be my friends
From the magical place,
Could they???"
And immediately upon that thought being thought,
A familiar foggy mist rolled in behind them.
She would never be the same.

27 Droplets of Time

In times like these,
We ask you please,
To be the sole observer
Be still and witness
Who you are,
In every faceted moment.
Be still to feel the breath of time,
Move in and out and through you.
Be still and truly take it in,
Upon the sighs in motion.
The true exhale,
The full release,
Of empty and of full.
Behold the sunlit drops of time,
Of love, of joy, of splendor.
Just breathe them in
With each inhale,
Absorb their every fiber
Into your being,
With form unseen,
The common IS uncommon.
With dancing swirls
Of light between,
Connects our sunlit droplets.
The purist sound,
Of Truth resounds,
Between our sands of time.

28 The Colors of Your Voice

With those of you who feel the sea
Swirling and whirling inside me,
For all the trials you've yet to see,
I give my love to you.
With all the speaking without words,
There's time to see and heal the hurts,
With every song you dare to sing,
I share my words with you.
In every morning of the Spring,
You'll hear its tone through everything,
With colors bright both day and night,
We give our hearts to you.
The flower that has yet to bloom,
The asteroid shower that's coming soon,
In times of hope, in times of joy,
We sing these words to you.
Each breath of hope,
Each step so brave,
We tear the bars from every cage,
To realize that through our eyes,
They aren't there at all.
Each breath of hope,
Exhales the truth,
In color and in tone.
In pinks and blues and greens and gold.
Exhale the truth through colors.
They swirl around, right through the air,
Envelop me and you.
These words of truth, they linger strong,
Releasing clouds of rainbow,
Into the air for all to see,
They glisten, and they glimmer.
They leave a mist of love and joy,
Your colored words remain.

And as the day, it ticks on by,
Perceiving time in motion,
If one should happen, through the way,
To cross these words and colors,
Well, may they brighten all those days,
That cross into its path.
For walking through these greens and blues
And pinks and reds and golds.
Amidst the morning sun and dew
And colors bright and new.
Even for the grumpiest of the journeyers today,
Will breathe these colors through the lungs to every of their cells,
And have the choice to start anew,
Oh, what a gift to give!
So, with each thought, each word, each sound,
An energetic vessel.
With signature unique and true to how you feel each moment.
Choose wisely your experience,
For its not just for you.
The words and thoughts and energies,
You have here on this plane,
You share with each and every being,
In every single day.

29 Pools of Consciousness

Your tale grows forth, each passing day,
Release imagination.
For that is all that limits you.
Here in this third dimension.
As it rings through your every cell,
Yet underneath awareness.
Directing when and where to go.
It then becomes your master.
Look in your pool of consciousness,
Look deep into with wonder.
When you are still,
So is the pool,
Reveals to you its secrets.
And if you stay, with still some more,
You'll sink down through its layers.
Collecting bits you've left behind,
Of memories gone by.
Observe them here, beneath the surface,
No need to shout or plead.
Be gentle with them floating there,
Ask them what they need.
In times of woe, in times of strife,
A part of us remains.
Below the surface of the pool,
Struggles to reemerge.
Approach them kindly and with care,
They're delicate and frightened.
When poked or prodded,
They squirm away, not knowing what to do.
Extend a hand of love and peace,
To memories down there.
For when they squirm, the ripples reach,
All corners of your pool.
Offer the bits, of times gone by,

An outstretched hand of love,
Forgiveness, peace, and calmness deep.
For only then you hear them
They'll tell you what they need from you,
Perhaps it's just a hug.
Each tired bit, will realized,
It's still a part of you.
Cradle them near,
Your heart my dear,
Hold them and rise together.
No separation anymore,
Between these bits and you.
You reach the surface,
Bright and new.
A deeper understanding,
And with these insights
From the bits of memories gone by.
You see your image, brighter now,
Reflecting back at you.

30 Hope of Grace

The hope of pure grace
The pure grace of hope
The grace that we are
And that we hope to be
As hope we lift
As grace we shine
Across the sunlit mornings
Today it's hope and grace we find
Beyond the waves of love

31 Be Still With Me

Sparks fly in the heart, rivers in the mind.
Today is but a moment we have in time.
Stay with me here, and be at peace.
Stay with me here, be free and ease.
In times of joy in times of sorrow,
When you think there's no tomorrow.
Is where you see the strength you'll need,
And with the true emotions lead.
For many times you'll say and hear,
The times with which your timings near.
Of all these things you'll have to borrow,
In times of strength, in times of sorrow.
For none of this exists, my dear.
It's all inside, betwixt your ears.
Align with truth, align with love,
Since you are with me, here above.
We're everywhere, we're everything.
The past, the future, the unseen
And as you dream your dreams and thoughts.
We sit together, in the rocks.

32 Songs From the Universe

This timeless journey throughout time,
Encourage cells to waken,
For organs and limbs and beings to wake,
Upon this crystal morning.
The waking of each part of you,
Will bring with it times knowing.
And as these parts of you awake,
Allowing structured movement.
Awaken too the tones of life
That swirls within your cells.
The swirling energy of life,
Will mix and move within you.
Without you too, surrounds each being
In infinite connection.
This swirling energy of life,
Takes many different forms.
Takes colors and tones
And shapes and movement and thought
Of every living being.
Those things you see that do not seem
To be alive to you.
The rocks, the water, air and soil,
Magnetic waves and more.
For everything you know and see
And hear and feel and touch.
Carries with it swirling life,
On good days and on bad.
They hold for us
The constant love,
We feel it every day.
And if you listen close, my dear,
To rocks and trees and mountains,
They'll share with you the frequency
Of life and liberty.

They'll tell you what you're made of,
Same energy as them
They'll tell you why you're here on earth,
To experience the beauty.
To appreciate all that is with AWE,
And share it with you neighbors.
To listen to the songs they sing,
Each rock each sea each planet.
These sounds of life will resonate,
Each tone a little different.
Each tells the story from its view
A slightly different color.
Creating hues and melodies
Of life each day for you.
In concert with each living being
That's here upon this earth,
Sing harmonies of stars and planets
And galaxies alike.
With every day,
You choose to hear
Songs from the universe.
You realize
And close your eyes
The melody is you.
With every note you choose to sing
With every bit of you.
From cells to organs and to limbs,
From every part of you.
From thoughts and emotions in your being,
From actions and behaviors.
For every expression of your being
Participates in song.
For when you choose to listen close,
You also choose to sing,
From every of your fibers.
Rings true the songs of earth and sky

And all humanity.
Creating endless harmony,
The universe, she sings!

33 The River

This constant flow of love and light
Is where we start our journey
In tears of joy we densify
Withholding nothing
Only love.
Whole as we are, we plummet through
The dimensions of space and time,
We choose to forget.
Why do we choose to forget? You may ask
Because, oh the joy of remembering!
As paint covering a brilliant masterpiece
Peels and cracks
Revealing just a glimmer
We start to see.
Looking at this masked gem straight on
May not reveal its truth.
But when you tilt it into the light
To peer into the crevasses,
The glow of wonder and awe ignites!
What could it be, hidden beneath,
This thick and gloppy coating?
Perhaps its gray to make you think
It's plain and ordinary.
"Nothing spectacular to see here, look away!"
It says to you each day
And as your journey
Runs its course,
With all your time and motion.
The thick gray coating
Chips away
Creating timeless portals.
What's that you see between the cracks?
Its poetry in motion.
The swirls of endless harmony,

Of color, of sound, of light.
This glorious river of creation is there
In constant motion
Transforming and transitioning
Through ebbs and flows of tide.
This tidal river flows inside,
In all of your directions
Reflecting what you're here to see
Beyond the sands of time.
"Oh, what beauty!" you may say
Once you can get a peek.
And try to see some more through force
Of tearing at the paint.
The gray and gloppy paint resists,
Its clutching to its purpose.
Obscuring vision,
True and clear,
Making it hard to see
The beauty that we truly are
Between the cracks of paint.
And finally,
One day you wake,
Decide to stop the struggle.
You've fought too long
To cross the veil,
Of gloppy gray paint cover.
It's in that moment,
Motion stops,
The paint globs stop their holding.
In absence of your fighting words,
The pushes and the actions.
The paint has naught to push against,
In stillness it relaxes.
And as the glops of paint relax
Into a peaceful slumber,
They curl up into tiny balls

Of light and fluffy specks.
It's in this moment
As they rest,
In peaceful timeless slumber,
That with a breath
You blow away
The dust of obscurity.
With open stillness look again,
Into the frame once more.
For now, you'll see what lies beneath,
A glowing constant journey.
Of swirling color, light and tone,
Creation, life and beauty.
When diving through the depths untold
Of this swirling tidal river
Remembering the tide is you
And you make up this river
These colors, tones and light
Are you
They make up everything.
Comprising you, your struggle through
Each day with globs of paint.
This light and tone and color too,
Have made up everything,
Including those gray glops of paint
That shriveled into dust.
Were part of you, your path, your journey
To get right back to you.
Appreciating, once again,
In self-discovery,
The flow of beauty, joy and love,
That make up everything!

MY WISH FOR YOU…

May everything you do be a song.
May every song you sing be from your heart.
May your heart always be filled with Love.
May you share your Love freely with all you meet.
May the Love we share reach every soul, across this blessed Earth.
May every action, thought and being share in Love's brilliance for eternity.

You are a song from the universe. Never stop singing your song!

www.ingramcontent.com/pod-product-compliance
Lightning Source LLC
Chambersburg PA
CBHW071504070426
42452CB00041B/2284
* 9 7 8 1 7 3 5 7 1 2 1 1 6 *